The Poem Stands on Its Head
by the Window

poems by

Bonnie Maurer

Finishing Line Press
Georgetown, Kentucky

The Poem Stands on Its Head by the Window

Copyright © 2023 by Bonnie Maurer
ISBN 979-8-88838-341-4 First Edition
All rights reserved under International and Pan-American Copyright Conventions. No part of this book may be reproduced in any manner whatsoever without written permission from the publisher, except in the case of brief quotations embodied in critical articles and reviews.

ACKNOWLEDGMENTS

Publisher: Leah Huete de Maines
Editor: Christen Kincaid
Cover Art: David Freemas
Author Photo: Jessica Freemas
Cover Design: Elizabeth Maines McCleavy

Order online: www.finishinglinepress.com
also available on amazon.com

Author inquiries and mail orders:
Finishing Line Press
P. O. Box 1626
Georgetown, Kentucky 40324
U. S. A.

Table of Contents

1.

Clearing the September Garden 1

That Summer, A History 2

What Happened to the Hickory Shades Motel 4

Love, War and the News, 2002 5

In Today's Paper 6

Midwestern Elegy 8

Mother and Daughter Still Life 9

This Remission 10

2.

Swimming with the Rabbi at the New Year 15

Tiny City of Remembrances 16

At The Mah-jongg Table 18

As It Is Said 20

Wrecked Devotion 23

No More "Old-Country" Jewish Grandma 25

In Rohall's Diner 27

3.

Himmler's Lunch in Minsk, 15 August, 1941 31

Breaststroke 32

The Survivor's Story 33

Second Generation: Ticket to His Father's Nightmare 38

Dorit's Story: In My House the War Did Not End in 1945 40

Forgiveness 43

Searching for the Warsaw Ghetto 44

Treblinka Extermination Camp/Museum of Flight and
    Martyrdom 46

On This City Bus to Auschwitz 48
Auschwitz-Birkenau Tour 49
Our Lunch in Warsaw, 10 September 2012 51
Buy a Hasidic Jew for Your Souvenir 52
Jewish Star 54
Remember 55

4.

At Last 59
What an Afternoon is Here 60
The Terra Cotta Old Women 62
The Poem Stands on Its Head by the Window 63
Acknowledgements 65

For David and Jessica

1.

*"Because each of us tells
 the same story
 but tells it differently."*
 —*Lisel Mueller*

Clearing the September Garden

uncombed as my daughter's hair—
flowers appear, curls twist at her shoulders—
we pull the tangle of bean and squash vine.
Yarrow, sun-gold healers, burns brown,
pungent as the old herb books with stories
of women who knew how to heal, how to
bury the fingernails of a sick child or
advised to turn the picture against the mirror
of the lover gone sour.

Thick stems lean into the cool circle
pines make, the place we sit,
and I tell her the tale of the Indian maiden
who ran from her false lover to the arms
of the evergreen.
"Yarrow, sweet yarrow…" begins
the chant the maidens sang
to ask a vision of their future lovers.

I cut daisies and zinnias, faded
as summer dresses,
the dead yarrow blossoms,
and toss the stems
my daughter throws into the compost pile
casting another spring.

What of this wild cleome? she asks.
Sticky white starlight wands,
or my white hair,
all summer claiming the wind,
waving on long stems as if
risen from the ancient sea:

"Leave them," I say.

That Summer, a History

That summer I wore tea rose,
        the cheap perfume. My daughter
                      pressed her arms to my wrists,
    we floated in that wind to the yard
                      to the garden swing—one yellow rose.

That summer before, I lost the milk song,
        the baby wrapped in gypsy cloth, scarf
                      my grandmother sang of another summer
    before the war, black river and
                magenta roses knotted on her chest.

The baby tugged at my breasts and drank
        each blossom free as I thought of ladders and
                      twisted the gypsy cloth fringe under
    and over my fingers like the prayer
                shawl strings I used to wind
    around my hand as a child
                until I could climb
    its silk string ladder,
                a traveler.

That summer I lost the cornucopia of my lover's hands.
        The space shuttle launched, progress sparked
                    the skies—magenta blooms. The horizon
    divided our desires.

That summer my cousin the astronaut
        became the name on a silver bridge
                      and I lost the lover
    who pulled me from the dreamwater,
                  who loved to speak of the dollar
    lost at nine from the Sisters of Precious Blood,
                his early lessons learned in their silver roulette
    wheel spinning, and in the relentless
                keel of his father's heart.

That summer before, my brother wanted
        to leap like the fish, like the long, lake pike
                my father pulled to the boat all those
    dawn-light summers.
              And how my brother looked upon
    his father's heart the way every morning
              my son and I would look with wonder to see
    if the heron stood in the river shallows.

That summer I lost one imagination.
    The dinosaur my son pulled by his father's belt
             across the bedroom floor to Chicago
    to see the skyscrapers. He pulled us all
             across the sea-foam carpet—old bones—
    we would get there.

But not my sister.
    Wherever we went
             strolling together,
    combing our hair,
             I promised my sister
    goldfinch on the honey locust, taste of
              lavender in the iris,
    and into the weathered barn, the black
              boots and silver spurs luring me,
    I lost her by my father's kiss.

That summer at the lake,
    where the bluebird returned her weave,
              lily pads, gods' burnished hearts,
    led like footprints from the water's edge,
              and I made myself into a pocket
    for grief, shawl for comfort,
              cloth for the table—
    the place we begin again:
              ripe strawberries in a blue dish,
    loaf of bread and serrated knife.

What Happened to the Hickory Shades Motel

which I would paint in Cezanne squares—
ginger orange, mellow coral, chalk
blue—and to those metal chairs by the doors—luminary yellow—
we slouched in, you and I, new lovers? Remember
the two of us waking at dawn to an ordinary autumn,
kicking sycamore leaves brown and broad as mitts,

and the geese lifting off into high sky—with the fly balls!
—baseball, not even on our minds, really,
out here rocking in those two metal chairs
attached by their hips and armrests some ghosts from the fifties
gave up for us, lovers, you and I, dangling legs, and mine
reaching over to your blue Levied lap?

I would hang this painting in the middle of nowhere
on the road's curve—bend in our thinking—together
we can do this, and we did. All
the orange maple leaves pointing to us,
nodding *yes* like the bobble heads of dogs
on the dashes of Corvairs in the 60's never quit.

This is the painting of the Hickory
Shades Motel you said *why?* to, and I said for the name,
the reason we eat a tangerine or kumquat,
now a still life, washed in discreet white,
now offering a free breakfast
and one white plastic chair out front.

Love, War and the News, 2002

I am brushing my hair in the mirror
for the chance meeting
with my lover at the dentist's office.
And I am thinking of pulling him
into the stairwell
before the dentist's door
and kissing him in the corner
and he will have no part of this and I will be
stuck standing on the Midwest flats
of the stairwell in my own film-noir fantasy.

The man I am passing on the way to the dentist
is picking his nose enthusiastically,
and I am reading a poem in my car
about Midwest romantic bullshit. (I still want love
and still don't know how to get it.)
Love always wags
its betrayal tossing up
fool's gold and dust behind,
and you can quote me
on that for your country song.

My mouth open: wide, wider, widest.
I leave before my lover's appointment.
It is January 2002: India stuffs land mines
into the patchwork of its Pakistan border,
batting for the newest peace quilt.
And the sad lion,
and his zookeeper, Mr. Omar,
in Kabul, stare back.
Mr. Omar must decide who
is going to eat,
he and his seven children
or this lion,
one-eyed from a grenade blast,
king of all of us, beasts.

In Today's Paper

On Sunday in Indiana, Dimitry
Popov tried drowning in the White River.
He threw his violin in first.
It rose, singing for Chagall
into an azure sky.

Popov had strolled at the zoo with his violin
among elephants on a gray day,
dipping as a goldfinch in flight
among round tables of tea
and mustard-yellow tea cakes.

Popov had asked for requests from the children.
He strummed the twinkle of a star and
the grunts of pigs. His tarantella
stirred the summer current
while flamingos across the river
stood on one foot, espousing
the prophet Hillel: If I am not for myself,
who is for me? If I am only for myself,
what am I?

Even the lemurs
of Madagascar (incidentally dying out),
lying at the feet of flamingos in Indiana,
languished in their reason,
swung their tails to the sweet notes
of traveling laughter.

But Popov, caught between his own melody
of joy and sorrow, left his blue Chevrolet
Chevette, climbed the guard rail
on New York Street and jumped
into the chilly waters of White River.

Moments later he disappeared
into the black river channel

careful not to touch
the Delaware swimming
in their outfits of melted crayons.

Gustafson, the diver, leaped
to the center of the river like a raindrop
in the concentric circles of the holy.
"It was just a matter of holding on to him," he said,

until Popov arrived at the amusement park
to do it all again,
of fresh air, of neon bright,
of couples strolling along the calliope.

Midwestern Elegy

What this highway has left standing are cemetery stones,
white and pocked as bones rising for markers;
the wooden bird, arms flapping in this wind: clack/click, clack/click.

The road is a gentle curve beyond—what you've seen a thousand times—
thin white arm of sycamore, then one field startles you with green.
The farmer's new silos will be there forever,

now the measure of flatness, and what you've heard today—
the skeletal remains of a girl, twenty,
found. Blackbirds swarm to the wires.

Cornstalks bend at the knees.
The last barn you pass gapes at you
holy and with its teeth out.

Mother and Daughter Still Life

"The world begins at a kitchen table." Joy Harjo

Opulent eggplant and ivory mushrooms
tossed in intimate friendship

with celery, green as summer rain,
circles of amber-skinned onions,

fat orange carrots, peppers, slick lobed
yellow and red: I paint vegetables

possessing the white-paper sky.
Then I turn to mother

for what she knows as an artist
and hand her my constellation.

Mother adds across our page a line
for the kitchen table where we sit. As if her brush

sweeps up sunlight, she braids gold rays
in and under, weaving two circles together.

For what mother knows of gathering a child's bounty,
she hands back our still life:

"Constellation of vegetables
in a basket on the table."

This Remission

We discuss who gets what.
I want Mom's old Mixmaster,
my sister—the green marble table.
Who gets the giraffe
collection on five shelves?
And I search my own shelves
for vacancy flashing,
like perusing the neon
hotel signs on the Miami strip
as a six-year-old in the family car
on vacation where we ended
up at the Driftwood Motel—
which fits this remission
where we stay with mother now,
lodged on shore
before we are licked wet
and tumbled back
to spin on the tongue
of a vigorous sea.

      2.

Mother has tossed her
yellow wigs for hair
grown back, white
as the noon sun on the water,
white as the tabletop
she continues to deck.
She taught us this much:
Order. And set the table
ahead of time.
"No matter how
prepared you are,
there is always
something," she says.

3.
Many, I say.
My sister has put
her name on
masking tape strips
and affixed one to
the Chinese tea set,
the rose vase, and
the Australian Aboriginal carvings.
A house divvied up,
mother laughs,

But already she
has divided us up,
handing me a new book
beginning with my baby
footprint inked 1949
on a white card,
and the photo
in my aqua suit
at the Driftwood Motel
where I joined excursions
to the parrot jungle
and the clown divers.

4.
This remission
let the squawking birds fly in,
the clown divers to begin their antics.
Let death and its diligent entourage
sit in the bleachers waving,
entertained, before
they come begging her for lunch.

Cavalierly, mother salts
popcorn for hers,
living among paintings
of boats at sea,
trees, mountains, fuchsia

orchids on the table,
silk kimonos, and pink
glass giraffes I may
have found a spot for.

2.

"What can I possess,
But the history that possesses me."
—Alicia Suskin Ostriker

Swimming with the Rabbi at the New Year

Forgiving is the way to an open field,
a life of birds in your heart.
You walk this path down to the lake,
singing. Turtles slide from their logs.
It is no secret you are here.

Remembering Moses and his thirst
in the wilderness, you enter
with a splash, water laughing out loud.
You are one God swimming in God.
The water frees your pockets,
bathes you in the promise
of a clean life, takes you in
the way a psalm opens your voice.

What is the name of God
but the sound of your own breath.
Frogs leap from lily pads.
Fish hover in their shallow pools of light,
and the seeds—free to multiply—
scatter the water on their journeys.

You dive under the unrelenting current
of Holocaust and hate.
Submerged in the mud—roots—
that connection, that tangle,
epiphany of root, stems
that lead you to the water lilies
floating under the sun.
Each green face uplifted, blazes.

At the shore, the blue heron stands on one foot.
You find your balance ("If not now? When?"),
emerge with your name intact.

For another year,
the water strider will guard your going out,
your coming in.

Tiny City of Remembrances

      1.   Say the butterfly in me flits to the lavender blossoms.
I ride that purple shudder down their spines.
          And summer is that sunshine song daddy sang to me.
He taught us all "My Island Goat,"
          coughing up the red scarves, flagging
the train—just in time. Cows on the track—
          his harmonica mooing—did not make it,
and his harmonic sound ran together: hamburger.
          But that goat
that Island goat—where no man is—but a woman
          stands there often and alone and eating quiet grass
and looking for that bridge
          because, believe me, there is a troll.
No telling his secret hands where I refused
          to give a shudder or sigh or sunshine song.

      2.   So, what's another dream of water
mean when I sink into depths
          like a bowling ball or find the dingy pigs
in the pond bottom, and I must avoid
          their bristles like Grandma's Fuller Brush
Man's wares. Or driving down the dirt road, all at once
          lifting over the sea in a red convertible, the silvery
 sailfish crisscrossing my head, (Look, I can almost touch them.)
          when I discover I only have to
lean to turn the car
          and land on shore at the old brown hotel?

I remember once, Chaim waited on the sand
          in his army fatigues.
Then life was good and I wore
          my blue Gottex suit in the Red Sea.
But this was not dreaming.

Yesterday, I made a running dive into the pool
          and a whale rose to the surface
like a slow elevator beside me.

3.   Mother pulled the bacon from my throat
like a mother bird in reverse, saving me at five.
            She never sang "Innocence is Not an Option,"
because she could not carry
            a tune in a hand basket as she says,
because nor can anyone find those words
            in any song, and never mind,
I am still the one at nine or ten who ran
            to the door with my piggy bank
offering pennies to whomever asked.
            And when my father looked at me
and said how do you know
            they are who they say they are, I stood
inside that question mark, innocence
            mine to savor silver as the full moon behind clouds.

Mother, who spun the Lazy Susan on the table,
            planted the butterfly bushes, bathed her pulse
in Youth Dew, one day, doctored her drooping eyes.
            I dabbed the blood and told
her a mythic tale of Isaac sacrificed as a young girl
            and headlong we tumbled
down the mountain together.
            Mother, who said she was sorry.

Mother, whose long toes with the red polish
            I rub now with Ponds Cream as if this lotion
of generations could soften all betrayals
            (I forgive you both).

Mother, who closes her eyes at 95,
            dreams down Broadway and Park
skimming in her roller skates
            with the rubber wheels
her father bought her,
            skate key around her neck,
opens all the doors in the tiny city of remembrances,
            to leave me
awake in the flooding sun.

At the Mah-jongg Table

"Mah-jongg is a game and tradition that transcends time." Celeste Heiter

Mother slid tiles to June, Harriet, Alice,
and Lee, the foursome who followed her life
Thursdays at noon until each passed away.
Alice, determined to return, flickered the lights
over their game a dozen times. (They said
as her husband's remarriage vows began,
the blue car that knocked down the light pole
in front of her house and moved on smooth
as butter was her last hand.)

In the picture window of America,
Mother waved her hands over Sabbath candle flames,
stormed the PTO when John Birchers tried to ban books,
invited the neighbors in to feast on latkes.
On 8-millimeter film, her Old-Spice-hubby
spliced their kiss with the bomb.
In the mailbox, she got her yearly game card,
pored over new hands and rules.

Mother backed down the ranch house drive
in her station wagon and the ladies moved on
to the Jewish country club—not allowed to join
other clubs in town—where they took up golf, cleats

clicking time before lunch
and their Thursday game began: 3 crak, 5 dot,
6 bam, clacking tiles until home. Mother
shook for me her coin purse,
jingling quarters won like a castanet in the air.

Mother played her hand through casseroles
and cocktails, through rumaki to sushi,
through humid summers thick as lemon meringue,
winters white as Pillsbury frosting,
and February, that sweetheart month

of death shrouds year after year,
flipping by like calendar pages on a movie screen.

Everyone knew
June's husband, the heart doctor, was having an affair.
"I am just unlucky," June said before she died
 of heart failure.

Then Harriet, then Lee,
wheeled off to nursing homes,
bent heads to loose-dressed laps.
Mother's beaded coin purse—
a hungry mouth open on the dresser-drawer.

So, I ask her how to play this game.
She clicks the butterscotch tiles,
arranging dragons, dots, flowers,
bams and craks, jokers—"with a bit of luck"—
she says at 95, and the four winds—constant
as main street through her American dream.

"Mah-jongg," Mother says, "It was a game I could play.
It didn't matter whether I won or I lost."

As It Is Said

elegy to Uncle Jack

"What's goin' on around here?"
you boomed your signature call
into our lake cottage,
and the screen door slammed. The yolk sun
quivered in your gas-house eggs, ready
when we clamored downstairs.
You fried up the perch for lunch, liked
your ptcha made from gelatin and calves' knuckles,
gefilte fish mixed from the carp
we caught with your licorice dough balls
rolled between our fingers at the pier.
Uncle Jack, you chewed on Cuban cigars
and I remember the odor of our cottage
when you were gone.

Oldest of seven, you left the house
when your father's old-country ulcer
burst, married Estelle of the elegant
silver streak in her hair,
and left your four brothers
your striped pants and suspenders,
your mother and two sisters,
depression glass and
short of cash.

I only heard how you heaped your plates
with lox and bagels, silver herring
in cream, sturgeon
and smoked fish flecked gold.

Legend of the get-rich-quick
scheme, I was told, but
not like your brother,
"High Dollar Dave"— not allowed
in our house for good reason,
Mother said, who could talk

the pants off a deal and did
with cars and women,
who, so charismatic,
could cheat a person twice and did.

You pushed Avantis, fit wigs, swore by bracelets,
sold aloe vera you insisted we rub
into our palms as the new cure all,
plied us with your vitamin pills,
popping in our bellies
like Mexican jumping beans
as we ran for the school bus.

Peddler to the end,
you drove that broken-down blue Ford
selling table pads, and measured one
for me as a wedding gift, then drove
into our alley to inspect the vines.
Our garden gave up pudgy, ripe
tomatoes to your pull and pail.
As if I were a tomato as a teen
you wanted to squeeze me
and did: "Hello Dear,"
your wet lips smushed
into mine.
I learned to duck
and dodge at a ripe age.

But Uncle Jack, how you crooned
"Embraceable You"
when the spoons chimed the glass
and your daughter kissed her bride

at her lesbian, Jewish wedding.
You stood and sang even to be thought a fool
by your own brothers shaking their heads.
On High Holidays you sang
from one end of the temple row,
your younger brother from the other.
On a seesaw of notes,
I balanced in between.

As one of ten, at the morning minyan
you counted, as they did on your kitchen-savvy
for lox & onion omelets and corn beef hash.
Uncle Jack, you missed your calling:
ten recipes in the House-of-God cookbook.

Your prowess with knife and fork
renowned, you could eat the world
and you wanted to and did
until your belly grew like Succoh's moon.
Uncle Jack, what was starving in you?
What you craved might be the answer for us all.
"Hi Darling," you said
at the last Passover table, hardly able to see
through thick glasses and over
your belly, your Passover plates, circling them
around you like the Israelites encamped in the desert.
"Pass the horseradish, will you, Estelle," you said, never
missing a word, spooning the hot, rosy relish
onto your plate of gefilte fish.
"Sh' ne' emar," you echoed your younger brother
singing at the other end of the table.
"Sh' ne' emar." "As it is said."

Wrecked Devotion

For Uncle Mick who regaled us with sevens

He was God's number, number
seven, youngest of seven,
born on the seventh day, God
rested. Count his given name
to seven. He lived at Sev-
enty-seven Seventy-
seven North and rang the same.

Up at seven, he bought and
sold wrecked cars and parts. For fif-
ty-seven years, he walked straight
past his sign out front: Two cars
faced each other, crunched, in mid-
collision, his motto lit
above: "We Meet by Acci-

dent--Drive Carefully," but who
believed this better-than-get-
right-with-God sign would be his
fate that day he drove in a
funeral procession—the
story more fit as a bal-
lad sung. Hit broad side, they ex-

tricated him from the (I
can hardly say "wreck.") Stunned. Now
his body, wreckage, recy-
cled scrap: dust, bones, hair and teeth,
his wide grin and voice that still
repeats to me, "Hello, bon-
ny girl," his hands that shook yours

as if he hooked a fish and
the dirt my brothers shoveled
in to pack him down. Dead at

seventy-six, double sev-
ens were not his roll. We thought
he spun with Lady Luck, but
then death boasts the last number.

We stand in wrecked devotion.

No More "Old-Country" Jewish Grandma

whose mother hid her
down the cellar
in the pickle barrels
when the soldiers plundered,

who sang to her sisters
in that Russian village
and rose like a Chagall bride
over the sea to America

declaring that's the story
about the boat overandover,
pulling the pins of her bun spilling
the silver waterfall down her back,

wearing her stash of bangles
and sequined skirts,
whistling from the kitchen to the table,
an aproned teapot, short and stout,

dancing her made-up Yiddish
ditty *Shena Punam*
Zesa cup, circling
our daughter's head, our son's.

No more old-country Jewish grandma,
arm & arm on her double date
with America, revelers
together on the 4th of July

choosing the fireworks
of her rebirth: red, white
and blue, the color wheel
of our lives.

No more old-country Jewish grandma delivering
us from that *narrow place*
at the Passover table she set
with those burgundy glasses

catching the last light tossing
red shadows across the white cloth—
the Red Sea parting for us
to take our seats.

In Rohall's Diner

after a painting by Red Rohall

Silver stools line up
along the counter
like chorus dancers
about to spin. Enter
Betty and Jules
to take them for a twirl
on seats red as sweet-
heart candy.

Jack, the soda jerk,
swipes his towel at
their elbows propped, hands
hooked. He smiles and takes his
pen: "What'll you have
America in 1941?
Skyscraper Sundae,
Adam and Eve on
a Raft, Pig Between
Two Sheets, 'V' for victory
at all costs, innocence
fizzing in the glass?"

"Boogie Woogie Bugle
Boy" floods the juke.
The walls blaze yellow
as the hot summer
day. No one they know
has gone to war. Betty
has not yet delivered
their son while Jules learns
to drop bombs. Two straws
in a nickel Coke.
Jack waves so long.
Outside the diner
their Buick grins—all
its chrome teeth shining.

3.

"Hear our story now.
…We are nothing without memory."
—Vedem

Himmler's Lunch in Minsk, 15 August 1941

(from his diary and excerpt on the museum wall at Terezin)

What did he eat for lunch
in the Lenin House, the SS headquarters,
at 1400, just after attending the morning
Einsatzkommando squad boys
taking turns to execute Jews near Minsk,
where reportedly brains splashed his face,
and he turned a greenish shade of pale?
And hey! he told the boys there,
terrible it all might be,
even for him as a mere spectator,
how much worse it must be for them
to carry the killing out and
he could not see any way around it.
"And reportedly he came to the view that it would be
necessary to find a more suitable and effective
killing method that would not have
such a disheartening influence on the executors,
particularly with women and children among the victims."
With what relish did he dig in his knife and fork? Was he
ravenous for lunch? With what eureka! This inspection trip—
the moment the gas chambers came into being.
With what hearty hale did he slug back his beer and lick his lips?

Breaststroke

Israel, Holy Day War, 73

In the kibbutz pool built by Germany's reparations,
I begin to glide through water, through his
story, hers: Rifka saved
under straw by the Polish peasant woman,
Yankel's life-saving scrap, Miriam's rape
and flight to the forest, Yitzak pulled away
as a child from his parents to England.
I begin again
through daily chores—
pruning lemon trees with Yitzak,
harvesting chamomile in Miriam's garden, attending
Yankel's cows, stirring cream
for Rifka's creations—because their sons and daughters,
soldiers armed to warring borders,
took leave, and I came to take their place.

I begin again
through his story, hers, through solace,
love, taste of bitter fruit,
through count-my-own blessings, ironing
their work shirts, washing dishes,
through the single, diligent
loneliness of my body in the pool,
sunlight refracting the water—cut
glass—shards of blue and green,
at night under red flares, under the moon,
my body a scissors, a knife, an arrow
shooting along the continuum—glide
and yes, glide and yes
glide through the fighter bombers'
sound of sky breaking.

The Survivor's Story

"Only with death in our eyes, can we seek a wild chance." William Pillin

      1.
He lives among us,
Meyer Bronicki, who can retell
what he said at sixteen
to his father, 1941:
"The Nazi killers have arrived."

He told his father, Fivel,
"Don't go,"
when the Nazis demanded
carpenters to set up their new camp.
His father would not listen.
He was not seen again.

Rounded up
with other Jews in the market,
Meyer, in his black Yeshiva cloak,
stood accused
of killing a German soldier.
The Nazi executioner cocked his gun
just as another ran in news of the guilty sniper.

For the next two months,
Meyer hollowed the dirt
under their lime floor,
scraping with spoons,
opening a place to hide.
Up to the ghetto wires,
he carried village dirt
of Dvorets in his pockets,
emptying as a Jew's life.

Two days before Christmas,
the Nazis surrounded the camp.
When they called the Jews out

of rooms they had been corralled into
many went, believing their ruse,
not Meyer. He had seen
the gentile brigade carrying shovels.
Why do they need shovels, he asked himself,
if all the Jews are going to another place?
"They were liars," he said. "The Nazi killers have arrived."

Meyer found the cellar
where his fellow Jews squeezed together
around a single candle flame.
Huddled in there would be more friendly, he thought.
We are crowded, a voice spoke to him from the dark.

And Meyer knew that was true.
He hurried back to their small room,
slipped his mother, Golda,
under their floor, arranged the beds over them,
and slid in, moving the piece of wood just so.
And when the Nazis barged inside,
stomping the floor, he could see their boots
through the cracks as they searched
for Jews in their room—
but not under beds.
Meyer and his mother held their breaths.

Three days passed until they heard
no more German sounds.
Meyer and his mother scrambled out
into a red reflection in the dark, fire
licking at the windows. The cellar door
hung ajar—friends and neighbors
slumped into that stone coffin.

Meyer and his mother ran to the fence,
pulled apart the barbed wire,
ran through fields
to the village of Ozerani
where the peasant woman, Manja

said *I cannot hide you. If they catch
me, they will burn down my house.
Go to the forest* and she shoved under his arm
a loaf of farm bread. Another farmer
thrust into his hands a pickaxe, a shovel and straw.

                        2.
In the forest, at the base of a spruce,
Meyer laid down to measure
from his Jewish toes
to his golden head of hair.
He clawed and dug the hard, cold
ground with the pickaxe and shovel.
And he dug until the hole fit his length.
And he dug four feet down. And he and his mother
pulled at the peasant bread and climbed
into the earth grave he laid with straw.
And it was good the first day and they were not dead.

They clung to the roots of the spruce
(and each other) and they were not dead.

And worms found the clothes on their backs
(all they had) and they were not dead.

And Meyer hid their grave bed
with leaves and a stump over the opening
for a door and they were not dead.

Their bodies grew immune to the cold winter,
10 below. They rubbed on snow to keep clean.

The taste of dirt was bitter and their breaths,
bitter, swirling their cracked lips,
visible as the ghosts of their past lives.
Or the taste of dirt and their breaths
were sweet—they were not dead.

And this is how they did not die
for 90 days and nights in their grave bed:
melting snow in a can for water.

And for Manja's bread,
Meyer tramped to the village
in the dark hiding his tracks under falling snow.

And Meyer did not plead for divine help.
He did not ask God
to spread the canopy
of peace over all.
At sixteen, Meyer lost
his orthodox hat
and gave up God.

    3.
Into their forest womb
spruce boughs drooped melting snow.
Fleas began to bite and bite.
Meyer and his mother emerged into spring
itching and scratching from their muddy hole

just when Manja told them
of a group who asked
to meet others hiding in the forest.
The next day Jewish partisans,
armed with rifles, led by Tuvia Bielski
riding on a white horse,
escorted Meyer and his mother
in a cart to a village home
for a meal and the night.

*We'd rather rescue Jews
than kill Nazi soldiers*, Tuvia told them.

Dirt-crusted and flea-bitten,
Meyer and his mother joined
the Bielski brothers in the dense forest, 1942.

4.

Now I sit with Meyer. Spring sun
warms us through his apartment window.
His accordion sprawls open beside his chair.

"Imagine," he says. "We built bunkers.
We had no nails.
We ate mushrooms, blueberries,
horse meat when we had no food.
We moved around the forest like animals.

Imagine, we didn't take a shower,
never brushed our teeth,
never changed our clothes.
We were without salt for three years."

"Imagine," he says. "We fought back.
More than one thousand
survived with me in the forest."

We watch his return to the village.
He stands inside the fenced-in memorial
to the 4,000 murdered. "Look," he says to the camera,
"Someone has been digging the graves."
"Could this be my brother's skull?"

Meyer lifts his accordion to his lap.
Hands trembling at 90, pushing on keys,
he sings to the last line his "Song of the Partisans."
"And our steps, as drums, will sound that we are here."

Ticket to His Father's Nightmare

"Pain transfers, whether you talk about it or not." Levi, Second Generation

Levi will meet you at the coffee shop
and tell you how his father's Holocaust story
fits into his days.
How he eats pickled herring
three times a week and dill
bean soup, stuffed cabbage,
to remember his father.
How his own passport
is always up to date. How he sits
facing the doors,
counting on escape like his father taught.
How he dreams his father's nightmares:

He walks on the great street of a city,
ticker tape raining to his feet.
Each color holds a number.
But he cannot do the math. He cannot add
the numbers appearing on his arm.
Like a movie, the city dims, pulls away.
He is tossing again
on the lice-infested straw,
feverish from Dr. Mengele's last TB shot.
Only a drop of water in his chipped cup,
crusted thumb-deep in bedbugs.
The black rat gnaws at his toes. He begins to shake.
He feels his body lifted. Wait,
He is alive. He is their evidence
thrown into a flatbed truck
on top of other bodies, stacked
like mailbags—his flesh hanging paper-thin,
flesh, no envelope for bones—
hurled down a mine shaft,
his body tumbles against rock.
Darkness covers the face of the deep.
He is his father's scream. No one can hear him.

But the Russian soldiers spot the Nazi's blast
at the entrance of the mine.
He is carried out.
Into light. In a Warsaw hospital. Dead
And resuscitated. He is his father's breath.
There *is* morning. *The first day.*

Dorit's Story: In My House the War Did Not End in 1945

Hitler, the silhouette in our shade.
Hitler, in the carpet of my parent's footsteps.

Hitler, in the bickering of mother's tongue: *"If it weren't for you, she said to me, we could have all been dead and I would not have had to come to this country."*

Mother was not in her right mind. When the Gestapo was not going to let her go, father said either we all go or we all die. I am not leaving my wife

and my child here. My great grandmother collapsed on the station platform. We get to Holland and miss our train connection to the ship.

Had we not missed the train, I would not be here. Everyone on that train was taken off and shot. When we get to the ship there is a ladder.

Father is holding me on the ladder. People are pulling him from the ladder and the ladder goes into the water. We were the last.

Hitler, in the fur machine sent here all the way from Austria.
Father fashioned fur coats until he was 88.

Hitler, in grandmother's Shabbat candlesticks on the mantel. Grandmother said first it will be bad then it will go away. This is the way it was for Jews.

Along came Hitler and my grandmother wanted to get us out. How was she going to get us out? She didn't know anyone in America. Had her house cleaner not

knocked the prayer book over, had the post card not fallen out with the address from the man grandmother had helped send to music school, I would not be here.

He had become a cantor in America. And she wrote to him and he answered, and he got my father a job as a furrier—in America.

My parents never resolved the loss of their families.
They sat on the sofa, grief tucked in the pleats of their soft hearts.

Hitler, in mother's apple strudel.
Hitler, in the bubble eyes of dish suds.

Hitler, clutched in the pockets of mother's fur coats,
zipped into her leather pocket books.

In my house, I became a swinging door. Outside
I grew up in America. I danced. I played piano.

I had no story to be stuck in. Inside, Hitler
tickled his mustache at the kitchen table,

invited to every meal, Friday nights
sucking the chicken bones dry.

***

At my own house, I remember
it was Rosh Hashanah.

I always had my parents here for dinner.
No sooner did my parents sit down

and my father would start,
Hitler this and Hitler that.

I stood up in front of my children,
in front of my husband.

Did you notice there is no chair here for Hitler?
He was not invited to this meal.

He is not going to be invited to any other meal
and that was the end of that.

That's how it was.
When they left, all I could do was cry and cry.

***

Before mother died, she looked at me and said, *"Are you my daughter?"* and *I said "yes,"* and she said, *"Will you forgive me? I was a bitter mother."*

I forgave her. That's how it was.
Hitler slammed the door behind him.

Forgiveness

> *"Forgiveness is for you, not for anyone else. Getting even never healed a single person."* Eva Kor

Eva Kor, A7063
burned into her left arm,
knows the weather of her heart:
Cold, shivering at ten.
Her living sky darkened
from the injections of Dr. Mengele,
Angel of Death at Auschwitz.
 "I must survive,"
Eva Kor vowed to herself.

For fifty years
fog glued the grit of her teeth,
storms clogged the marrow in her bones.

Her nightmares persisted.
Had she washed
her hands with the soap
that was her parents?

At 60, she stood again on the Birkenau platform-of-no-return,
where Mengele had pointed her aside with her twin.
She danced the rain in that misery
until the child of ten
let the old woman go.

The sky stopped pelting.
"Joy," cried Eva Kor
in fair weather.

"Forgive," she cries now
the power of that thunder.

Searching for the Warsaw Ghetto

I cross Warsaw streets with my dark images.
Ghetto walls up to ten feet high
topped by glass and barbed wire. You've seen them:
families, gaunt and ragged,
smuggling a child out for a beet or potato.
A woman shivering from typhus.
Heaps of dead bodies naked in wheelbarrows.
Boys' hands tunneling underground passageways
to live—maybe.

I ask the hotel clerk,
pressing my city map into his hands,
"Where is the Warsaw ghetto?"
"You are standing in it."
"You mean last night I slept
on the feather bed, lingered
in the shower, hot and cleansing,
in the Warsaw ghetto?"
"Yes," he says.

I have come to Poland
to seek Holocaust sites
as if the seventy-year-old news
were as fresh as the fruit tea
I sipped this morning
in the lobby, in the Warsaw ghetto.

Between apartment courtyards
I find a remnant brick wall,
lean in and link my body
to family history in Poland.

I stroll through Warsaw's lavish parks.
Who is complicit in the old faces I see?
Does the Polish gentleman staring
me down in the tram
see an obvious American Jew?

I ask one young waiter,
"Do you recognize Jews
on the street?" "What Jews?" he asks.

Late one night I stand
in the middle of Stawki Street
on painted white tracks. Here,
the drunk engineer loaded his steel
freight car to full capacity.
I step back between granite walls,
into The Umschlagplatz
Memorial—
collection point for 300,000 Jews
deported from the Warsaw ghetto,
taken to die in Treblinka's gas chambers,
pumping day and night.

I read out loud the symbolic
Hebrew names carved on the wall.

Oh ears, summoning voices jostling, shouting to be heard.

Treblinka Extermination Camp/Museum of Flight and Martyrdom

"Beneath the grass, mingled in the sand, lie the ashes of some 800,000 Jewish human beings...." Lonely Planet

No strewn brick of evidence: no
gas chambers, open-air cremation
pyres, no men going about their business:
shorning hair, shoving bodies in,
shoveling out, hammering teeth for gold.
Only memorial stones: one carved Never Again,
and the monument to Jews where gas chambers
once stood. This symbol of bodies burned—
a grid of basalt, volcanic rock, black-
hard as the order to kill, right, Commandant Kurt Franz?

"Beautiful Times" you called your scrapbook
of photos, Commandant Franz.
Ah, those were the days:
The crane for digging graves. *Click.*
Building for sorting valuables.
Storehouse for the Jew's property (disguised
as train station with clock and timetables). *Click.*
Barracks where women undressed. *Click.*
Approach to gas chambers
puffing out two thousand a day—

snip-snip, zip-zap,
you wiped your hands of that,
Commandant Mr. Kurt Franz.
Freight car to camp, gone in
two hours flat, as if
they never lived—gulped a glass of ale,
rubbed their sons' and daughters' heads,
shat, pissed or kissed,
discussed philosophy or math,
hummed in song, rocked in love.

On the sunlit path
the Jews have turned to stones,
stones set walking the Black Road,
stone shoulders shrouded in shadows,
bent in mourning. I walk with them
to gravestones—upheaval
jagged and sharp—among the buttercups.

On This City Bus to Auschwitz

1.
We choose window seats.
Pass the houses painted yellow
sporting red gabled roof tops—
patriotic as the Polish flag,
flower boxes drooping light-hearted
petunias at every window, and every
window framed by white curtains of lace,
fenced-in shrines to Mary,
willow trees and apple trees—full and plenty,
flat fields of corn, and in one
field, smoke visible in the air, something
burning clear. We pass the Wisla River
smacking its pewter lips in the sun.

2.
And for the ashes dumped by truckloads
into the Wisla River, rolling its singular shame
through Poland without song,
it takes a math problem: three
or four kilograms per person,
times more than one million murdered,
subtract the ashes spread onto local fields
as fertilizer, and how many kilos escaped to town?
Where do the ashes blow today—
into yellow paint? On the shoulders
of Mary? Into the apple dumplings?

3.
And we are told Nazis organized gardens
for flowers shipped to the Reich.
Imagine the young German bride
calculating her blissful steps down the aisle,
clutching flowers born from the ashes
of gassed and cremated Jews.
"I do," "I do," the bride and groom
vow above the floral scents
of roses, lily, baby's breath.

Auschwitz-Birkenau Tour

"You are visitors here, not tourists," the guide explains.

Down Block 6 hallway, we file
past the Germans' documented Jews,
tight-lipped faces posed, wallpaper of the perished.

The guide takes us to the glass-walled rooms:
human hair heaped, not yet sent
to the textile factory for making hair cloth—seven tons;
room of pots, bowls, spoons,
potato peelers; forty kilograms of eyeglasses;
and storm clouds of black shoes—
one red-buckled small as our palms.

We read aloud family names
chalked on tossed suitcases: Frank, Singer, Gottlieb, . . .
where keepsakes, packed for "resettlement"
were sent on, if not to the Nazis' girlfriends,
to the intended storehouse of an extinct people.

We follow the guide through Birkenau:
rusty train tracks crisscross the yard. And here
is the cattle car. Welcome to the death factory.
Unlock the bolt. Scream the door
open: the hunch and hush of nothingness.

We are visitors. Barbed wire
surrounding us is not electrified.
At the unloading ramp, a Nazi photo: bundled children
clutching dolls and bears. "Hurry,"
the guide mocks for us one commandant to the children,
"You will see your mothers that much sooner."
We follow him to the end
 of their short path.
"Remember your number," the mock commandant
admonishes, as we look
down into the changing-room pit, "so
you can find your clothes after your shower."

And there is no after.
We bend to our knees
at the gas chamber,
compelled to look back,
something in us turning to salt.

Our Lunch in Warsaw, 10 September 2012

So, we walk into a pierogi place in Warsaw
and sit at a corner table.
My husband orders Grandma's Soup
and I, pierogies filled with forest mushrooms.
I wonder, did the Jews hiding
in the Belarusian forest scavenge for such as these?

Can I eat in Poland without thinking about the War?

My husband's soup arrives. Fresh dill
afloat in the chicken broth. Yes, Grandma Pearl's,
he concurs. And the pierogies, delivered on a white
plate—purses from the moon crimped at the edges
just like the *kreplach* Grandma Martha fashioned.

Two teen waitresses in folkloric outfits
cavort in the doorway, leaning
and laughing into each other.
My husband and I eat in old-country grandma
heaven—Izrakapizra just on the other side
of Rugutka his grandmother used to say—
meaning nowhere now.

(Before WWII, the Jewish community in Poland was the largest in Europe and the second largest in the world—3.1 million in 1931. By 1944, Poland would become the largest Jewish cemetery in the world.)

Buy a Hasidic Jew for Your Souvenir

Krakow was to be a "Jew-free city." Hans Frank, 1940

Buy a Hasidic Jew for your souvenir,
and for your Polish friends
buy one holding a gold coin
to give the promise of wealth
and luck in their new homes,
as is the custom, I've been told.

In Krakow, shaped in clay and carved
in wood, Hasidic men play the bass,
accordion, clarinet and violin.
Can you hear them
in Auschwitz made to play?

Here Hasidic men dance
on display. Always their torsos
stretch long and thin, and
knees turn out like a dancing frog's,
arms reaching the sky in a wild gesture,
to God?

Choose the relics always smiling.
Many hold the Torah
with a breast plate of a Jewish star.
*When the scrolls were not
spit upon or trashed,
they were saved as treasure
of a burnt-out race.*
Look, the tallit dangling tzitzit
between their legs—
*Prayer shawls ripped
and cut in squares for rags—*

See how they huddle
together on the shelves,
wrinkled foreheads,

beards past their chins.
Always their black dot eyes
look at you sideways,
crazed. *Figure this.*

See them dressed
in black hats
and long black coats.
See them in striped pajamas,
shaved, tatooed,
or ashed.

Jewish Star

Not the yellow star
across their hearts—and hope
not to die—the Jews were forced
to wear,
this star I lift
from a black velvet cloth
affixed to a price tag
I can't afford. Petite pearls
trace one gold triangle.
Red stones, rubies or
garnets, trace the other.
What transport did this pin
take to arrive at this antique store
on a side street in Krakow?
I imagine the Jewish star belonged
to a young woman my age,
with children, and desperate
to hold on—the pin
her grandmother gave her mother
and her mother pressed
into her palm—perhaps
she sewed inside the lining of her coat.
I wish I could give this star a home,
take it to America and begin
a new arc: hand
to heart, heart to hand.
This pin still calls to me as I walk
down my street under the pearl moon.
I hope she sold this jeweled star
for the crust of bread to stay alive.

Remember

As if we want your breeze
to carry the crime forever

As if we want your river
to ride our ash

As if we want your ground
to climb our paths

As if we want your paths
to arrive at the light in our windows

As if we want your birches lindens
pines to weep

As if we want your stones
to heave our weight in your arms

As if we want your seeds
to sew our necklace of grief

Remember as if we want your breath
to taste us on your tongue

As if we want your tongue
to intertwine our names with yours forever.

4.

"Behind all this perhaps some great happiness is hiding."

—*Yehuda Amichai*

At Last

"It ought to be lovely to be old." D. H. Lawrence

So here we are
long teeth and gums
receding, but where,
into what universe?
Greetings, dry tributaries
camped around my lips
waiting for the salve of his kiss.

Hello creases in my forehead, formerly
the blank canvas—read joy,
surprise—now my flag
always rippling worry in the wind.

Good morning birds: Chickadees
waking in my knees,
it must be you singing,
long-legged shore birds
walking just under the thin skin of my hands.

And oh, arms and thighs,
as you slack into loose folds like silk pajamas
you are my Zen masters.
"Let go," you teach me,
even when I hold him tight.

Yes, buttocks, what fruit
does not sag as it ripens?
My halves of peach, no painter's still life.
I have heard age-old wisdom.
Now I know it is the ego's way
soothing the body, saving face.

What an Afternoon Is Here

Cape Ann

    We have found this Sunday afternoon,
you on the couch reading baseball statistics—hits,
runs, RBI's—and I, twenty love poems by Neruda.

    We have come to the edge of the sea. We love
and lick the salt from shoulders and cheeks and
the nameless channel above the lips,
the silver mica sand

    fallen on our thighs, stardust
blessed by accidents. I am not longing.
Yet my soul flies out over this sand and sea.

    Let the cormorants
pitch it back to the rocks where
I stand ready—your catcher,
your soft glove.

    I am not longing.
I only wish you would shout
your desire.

    You, who love baseball,
look at me making this up to you
while the whales are being sighted
only an hour away.

    Only an hour away, the Albanians
are calling Boston for the right way
to speak to God.

    Only yesterday another
worm crawled through Walt Whitman's
bones. (Who can call up the world for
love or despair?)

It makes no difference to me
who hits and runs. The sea is
infamous for winning every inning.

The Terra Cotta Old Women

Inspired by the clay women of Lea Majaro-Mintz, Israeli artist

For my daughter

Show up on this narrow street.
Enter the blue doorway. There is a place
for you in the artist's house. The terra cotta old women
sit on the porch, resting long arms atop their prominent bellies—
mounds of creation. Their breasts hang
out loud, full-bodied stories.
Stiff and conspicuously dressed, I find a seat
beside them on the stone ledge. The women bask
in their nakedness, unblinking, and stare
at the cameraman prepared to snap our picture.
Who would guess they ever had anything to hide.
Is this what we learn in old age? This is
who we are, the ladies want to say, but they chat
of other things and just sitting together,
mouths each a circle open in their conclusive joy,
I feel their camaraderie on this stone bench.
It is not too late to sit with them and learn
this lesson: unbutton, unclasp, uncoil.
I rise, as if I too am made by firm hands
with grit and iron and water, earthenware
fashioned to love and leave this space for you.

The Poem Stands on Its Head by the Window

Even so, the poem cannot reverse the order of things.
The fruit bowl on the table spills plums,
blue and speckled, still ready to split their skins.
Brains still blow up at markets and blood rains the beach.
Coins knock and jangle, clocks collide, and a buckeye,
polished as childhood, slides from the poem's pocket
into the rivered shag. Guns, bombs, missiles still fly in its head.
The poem's feet flex a silent beat. Can the poem move a line
of soldiers aimed to kill? Change a word to stop the genocide?
The poem sighs, heaves, utters the moans and sputters
of earth, the lost vowels groaning—hearts jettisoning
from daily life. The poem has seen the blue marble fully lit from space.
So, what gives, the poem asks, rearranging roots, hands and feet and blood and
breath to accommodate a world of violence and wonder? The poem
floats on a blue scribbled ground and ochre sky, reaches like Jacob's ladder.
When can the poem come down, walk among the pineapple groves,
tupelo trees, the coasts of Maine and Madagascar,
under the mottled green leaves safe again to marvel at you and me?

Acknowledgments

Grateful acknowledgment is made to the following publications in which poems in "The Poem Stands on its Head by the Window" first appeared:

Contemporary American Voices, online mag., "Searching for the Warsaw Ghetto," "Himmler's Lunch in Minsk, 15 August 1941," and "On This City Bus to Auschwitz"

Currents, 2017 Alexander and Dora Raynes Poetry finalist: "No More 'Old-Country' Jewish Grandma"

Flying Island, online mag., "This Remission"

Indiana Historical Society, Eva Kor exhibit, *"Forgiveness"*

Indiana Humanities Poetry Month website, "In Rohall's Diner"

Indy Writes Books, A Book Lover's Anthology, "Clearing the September Garden," and "What an Afternoon is Here"

Innisfree Poetry Journal, "In Rohall's Diner"

Jewish Post and Opinion, "Searching for the Warsaw Ghetto," "Buy a Hasidic Jew for Your Souvenir," and "Jewish Star"

Lilith Magazine, Charlotte Newberger Poetry Competiion, runner up, "As It Is Said"

Not Like the Rest of Us, An Anthology of Contemporary Indiana Writers, "Himmler's Lunch in Minsk, 15 August 1941"

Poetica Magazine, "Our Lunch in Warsaw, 10 September 2012" and "On This City Bus to Auschwitz"

Reconfigured, Finishing Line Press, "Swimming with the Rabbi at the New Year," "What an Afternoon is Here," and "In Rohall's Diner"

*So It Goes Anthology, Issue no. 3, The Kurt Vonnegut Museum * Library*, "The Poem Stands on its Head by the Window"

*So It Goes Anthology, Issue no. 5, The Kurt Vonnegut Museum * Library,* "What Happened to the Hickory Shades Motel"

The Wabash Watershed, online mag., "Love and War and the News, 2002"; "What Happened to the Hickory Shades Motel," and "Himmler's Lunch in Minsk, 15 August 1941."

The Wabash Watershed, Indiana Poetry Awards, "That Summer, a History"

Tipton Poetry Journal, "Midwestern Elegy."

War, Literature & the Arts, "The Poem Stands on Its Head by the Window"

The Mary Anderson Center for the Arts offered a retreat for writing and reflection where several of these poems were written.

Holocaust-related poems were composed under the auspices of the 2011-2012 Creative Renewal Arts Fellowship awarded by the Arts Council of Indianapolis and the Lilly Endowment to support travel to Poland and Israel. Interviews of Holocaust survivors and second generation were supported by an Individual Artist Grant awarded by the Indiana Arts Commission, 2015-2016.

Thanks to George Kalamaras, former Poet Laureate of Indiana, and Susan Bettis, feminist scholar, for their gracious devotion of time editing my work.

I am indebted to the dedication of my once-a-month Sunday poetry group these twenty-five plus years. And I cheer my husband Jeff for listening with his love and humor. Thanks to David and Jessica Freemas for contributing to the beauty of my book.

Bonnie Maurer holds an MFA in poetry from Indiana University. Her chapbooks include *Reconfigured*, Finishing Line Press; *Ms. Lily Jane Babbitt Before the Ten O'clock Bus from Memphis Ran Over Her*, Ink Press and Raintree Press; *Old 37: The Mason Cows*, Barnwood Press; and *Bloodletting: A Ritual Poem for Women's Voices*, Ink Press. Under the auspices of an Indy Arts Council Creative Renewal Fellowship, she composed a series of breast cancer poems culminating in, *The Reconfigured Goddess, Poems of a Breast Cancer Survivor*. In 2012, she was awarded a Creative Renewal Arts Fellowship to create poetry on her visit to Holocaust sites. Subsequently, The Indiana Arts Commission awarded her and Individual Artist Grant to interview Holocaust survivors. She has been nominated for two Pushcart Prizes and has been a finalist for the Indiana Poet Laureate. Maurer has conducted poetry workshops for the homeless in recovery, for the HIV+/AIDs affected/infected population. She continues to facilitate workshops for veterans and for the cancer community. Maurer is an Ai Chi (aquatic-flowing energy) instructor and currently, welds steel sculptures from recycled objects.

www.ingramcontent.com/pod-product-compliance
Lightning Source LLC
Chambersburg PA
CBHW020341170426
43200CB00006B/453